welcome
TO MY **World!**
Come Stay A while.

# welcome TO MY World! Come Stay A while.

FELICIA NOBLE WILLIAMS

 iUniverse®

# WELCOME TO MY WORLD! COME STAY A WHILE.

*iUniverse books may be ordered through booksellers or by contacting:*

*iUniverse*
*1663 Liberty Drive*
*Bloomington, IN 47403*
*www.iuniverse.com*
*1-800-Authors (1-800-288-4677)*

*Because of the dynamic nature of the Internet, any web addresses or links contained in this book may have changed since publication and may no longer be valid. The views expressed in this work are solely those of the author and do not necessarily reflect the views of the publisher, and the publisher hereby disclaims any responsibility for them.*

*Any people depicted in stock imagery provided by Getty Images are models, and such images are being used for illustrative purposes only. Certain stock imagery © Getty Images.*

*ISBN: 978-1-5320-9569-6 (sc)*
*ISBN: 978-1-5320-9570-2 (e)*

*Print information available on the last page.*

*iUniverse rev. date: 02/21/2020*

# Amazing

I'm Amazing!. You know it's true.

Are you acting like you don't have a clue.

From my incredible smile, the vibes that I give.

No care in the world. I only want to just live.

With my seductive eyes, they just make you blush.

Is it getting hot in here. Oh I feel very flushed.

You know I make you smile when I enter the room.

You better back up now, I'll have you jumping the broom.

I'm so amazing, I know you can see.

You know in your heart, you want to be with me.


Felicia Noble-Williams

# Are You The One

Are you the one who told me everything would be okay?

Are you the one that told me if I followed
God, trouble would never look my way?

who is the one that said "Dreams
Can Always Come True"?

Was it God who said "Good things will come for you"?

Is it right to think that God would
set you on the right path?

If you don't follow his rules, you will experience his wraft.

Setting a course and seeing it through
is a real important thing.

Reaching your goal and seeing your
potential, makes you want to sing.


Felicia (AKA) Feva

# Art

Paintings, Drawings are all a part of Art.

Wrap them, package them and put them in the cart.

I'm going to take them home and put them on the wall.

We are talking right now, but tomorrow I'm going to call.

If you wait for my call I won't be a bother.

I'll even throw in a picture of President Carter.

Felicia Noble-Williams

# Choices

The choices you make can make or break you.

It is something you want but not always like to do.

It gives you the opportunity to make
a decision on your own.

Your decision can make you a lot of
friends or leave you always alone.

The main thing is being happy with your
decision and standing by your choice.

Not forgetting it's your right, that you
are allowed to have a voice.

So make sure the decisions you make
are choices truly for you.

Just remember people are always watching
the moves you make, the things you do.


Felicia (AKA) Feva

# Colorful

It's a colorful day, I can see the rainbow in the sky.

The bears are looking for honey and
the birds are ready to fly.

A new season is beginning, the flowers
are starting to bloom.

The population is constantly flowing, I
hope the earth has enough room.

The bees are polinating the flowers and
the fish are swimming together.

This is such a great feeling. I wish it could last forever.


Felicia Noble-Williams

# Conquer Your Fears

To go through life not knowing what's to
come, could be a very scary thing.

For your heart to start racing and your body start
to shaking everytime the telephone rings.

To be waiting with anticipation for that telephone
call with good news at the other end.

Counting down the days, while you sit by the
computer, waiting for the moment to press send.

Thinking is this the right thing? Should you wait for two
more weeks? Should I give them just one more chance?

Then you press the button and you realize that it's
all over. In a heartbeat and at a single glance.


Felicia (AKA) Feva

# Cooking

Cooking brings me such happiness and joy.

I've been making things before my little boy.

Making cookies and breakfast
brings me such passion.

It's like a clothing designer in the world of fashion.

Donuts and cakes and so much more

Homemade goods taste better than a store.


Felicia Noble-Williams

# Curly Fro

Curly Fro I wonder if you are as happy as you look.

Standing here with your nose buried in your book.

Appearing very serious, the book must be good.

Not paying anybody attention. Acting just like you should.

Shutting out the world so you can concentrate.

Ignoring everyone like you're waiting for your date.

Curly Fro, your hair is making a statement.

Don't let me distract you, don't dare become complacent.


Felicia (AKA) Feva

# Fly Buttery Fly

The Butterfly has landed. It has found a new home to rest.

You have accomplished great things in life,
through the hard and many test.

God has called you home, to spread
your wings, my pretty Butterfly.

To soar like an Eagle and spread love and
joy through his beautiful blue sky.

So Butterfly don't forget me, when my time
comes, to soar right by your side.

For I will look for you when, heaven opens it's
doors, to meet me at the gate as my guide.

Felicia (AKA) Feva

# Free Spirit

Hey Free Spirit, where are you going?

To the Marina for some rowing.

and after that, where will you be?

On a boat across the seas.

Now tomorrow night, will you be home?

My friends want to go to Paris, maybe Rome.

Hey Free Spirit, are you going to the fair?

Not without a new outfit, and a new style for my hair.

Hey Free Spirit, what about the shoes?

To match my eyes, It's so hard to choose.


Felicia (AKA) Feva

# Good Day!!!

Good Day to all it's a beautiful morning.

The sun is peeping out, but it appears to be stalling.

Sun come on out! Everybody is waiting for you.

The skies are grey, but we need them to be blue.

People look so sad, they need to be cheered up.

We need dancing in the streets, so people grab your cup.

Get a drink of this wonderful life that we all hold so dear.

Lift our voices so loud so the whole world could hear.


Felicia (AKA) Feva

# Hey Little Mama

Hey Little Mama you're off to the races.

To hit all the stores and all the market places.

Are you going to pick up a turkey from downtown?

and a ham for tonight's dinner, if I could find one around.

Now don't forget to make the collard greens.

and a large side of those string beans.

You can't forget your famous Lasagna.

Make you want to cry for your mama.

And finish off with your potato salad please.

You have to make a lot for one bowl is just a tease.


Felicia (AKA) Feva

# How Do You Let Go

Letting go of your adult children is very hard you know.

When you look at them you still see
that little kid putting on a show.

Entertaining their families while
exploring the world around them.

Watching your children grow up to adults,
knowing they started from a stem.

Knowing all you want to do is protect
them and watch them grow up.

Making sure they enjoy all stages of their lives like
when they were little and get their first pup.

To be there through good and bad times, through ups
and downs, letting them see you'll always show.

I ask society, I ask the world, how do
you let your adult children go?

Felicia (AKA) Feva

# I want To Fly

I want to fly high as the sky would take me.

I want to soar far across the clear blue sea.

I want to soar like an Eagle spreading his wings.

I want to break barriers like glass,
when a Humming Bird sings.

I want to conquer my fears and not be afraid.

I want a job that is truly greatful to
have me and is glad I stayed.

I want to accomplish great things and walk across a stage.

I want bad people to leave me alone
so I could get rid of this rage.


Felicia (AKA) Feva

# Ice Cream

I truly love Ice Cream, it's one of my favorite desserts.

My sister loves ice cream too, but she prefers the sherberts.

I tried Sherberts before, they taste like icees to me.

With a little touch of ice cream, you barely can see.

My favorite is Chocolate, but Vanilla goes with everything.

No one is crazy about chocolate, so I
just go with the way they swing.

They seem to be crazy about Cookie Dough
and they love Cookies n Cream.

Sometimes they have me buy so much
of it, I simply want to scream.


Felicia (AKA) Feva

# I'm Back

I'm back where I belong. I did not leave without a trace.

I left you some of my best work so you
would never forget my face.

I'm a Poet- mind body and soul.

I will be one to the day I die. Touching
people's lives until I get old.

I think of things and put words together.

Like an Artist on canvas instead using paper.

My poems rhyme like rap songs

Flowing together like a pair of thongs.

Picking up food with such an ease.

My poems touches your heart and then it leaves.


Felicia (AKA) Feva

# It's My Birthday

Today is a special day. Do you know why?.

Because it's my Birthday, and I'm not that shy.

So pull back the covers, because it's that time.

To get things started and bust out this rhyme.

Because today, it's all about me.

It's my time baby, can't you see.

One day it will be, yours also too.

But today do not cry, Boo Hoo Hoo.

So just let me have a little bit of space.

I have alot to do, I must pick up the pace.

For tonight has to be right.

The Star is here. Now click on the lights.


Felicia Noble-Williams

# Mind Games

Why do people play Mind Games with
people they don't really know?

Don't they know you can't get over with intelligent
people because everything does show.

Why do people try to take others for granted,
like they don't possess feelings too?

Does this person sound familiar, does
this person sound like you?

Why do people go around and
purposely try to hurt others?

Not keeping in mind this could be your father or mother.

Why do people set out to destroy peoples spirit and joy?

Without thinking of the outcome of that little girl or boy.


Felicia (AKA) Feva

# Paradise

Welcome to our Paradise. Our aim is to serve you.

With a comfortable room and tropical drinks,
we change your grey skies to blue.

With gorgeous blue water and beautiful white sand,
we're guaranteed to put a smile on that face.

As you lay your head on the soft pillows and
sink your body into the exquisite big bed, all
worries leave your mind without a trace.

So come to our resort and let your hair down.
I'm sure we can help you unwind.

Just follow the laughter and the sounds of people
having fun and leave all your problems behind.


Felicia (AKA) Feva

# Peace

People search their whole lives looking for peace.

It's not something you can buy with the option to lease.

It is something for your mind, body and soul.

It is something that you strive for even when you get old.

Peace on earth and good will to all, is what we are taught.

This is something we learn, This is not
something that can be brought.

This is not something you can buy, it's
not something on the shelf.

It is not something that comes to you automatically.
It's not something that comes with wealth.


Felicia (AKA) Feva

# Red Hair

Pretty girl with the Red Hair.

How you make people want to stare.

Caught up in your book on the train.

Hope you have an umbrella. Looks like it's going to rain.

Don't pay me any mind, I'm just observing.

I'm use to intruding. I'm in the field of serving.

Go on with what you're doing. Don't pay me any mind.

The message you seek, I'm sure you will find.


Felicia (AKA) Feva

# Spring

Today is the first day of Spring and
you can't even tell it's here.

Flowers have not started blooming yet
and the cold chill is still in the air.

The North eastern is on its way for
the fourth time this year.

It plans to come up the East Coast and soon arrive here.

I'm tired of this weather, I wish that Spring would come.

I don't need everything now just plenty
of flowers and sun or just some.


Felicia Noble-Williams

# Stand up

It comes a time when we all need to stand up.

For our beliefs, for ourselves, sometimes
you need a push or a bump.

You can't just always go with the group,
when you know that things are wrong.

Sometimes you might have to stand
alone, but remember be strong.

It's times that you make choices that
goes against the norm.

Sometimes you have to make decisions
and just ride out the storm.

People are not always going to like you for
what you do or what you think.

Sometimes you have to ride the wave.
You can't just watch the boat sink.


Felicia (AKA) Feva

# Tunnels

My life is filled with Tunnels, some good some bad

Making a decision on which one to take
sometimes make me very sad.

Sometimes you think you picked the right
one and it turns out to be a dead end.

Sometimes they have you going in circles and then
you realize this is somewhere you already been.

I've spent my life trying to reach the top having
different hurdles just get in my way.

I know that hard work always pay off. I'm just
wondering when is it going to be my day.

It should not be this hard for a person, who
worked hard their whole life coming up.

This shouldn't happen to a person that does the
right thing, so don't get mad and tell me shut up.

It's time to take my rightful place amongst the senior staff.

Don't try to stop me or get in my way for
you don't want to feel the lords wraft.

For I'm protected by God as long as I follow
his path and take what is rightfully mine.

That day is coming soon for I feel it in my soul
and Oh Lord they going to see me shine.


Felicia Noble-Williams

# walk That Dog

Walk that dog. You know he is waiting.

Hurry up, the sun is fading.

He's going to want to go inside.

He's going to run and try to hide.

Dogs don't like the thunder and lightning too.

They can easily be scared. Just yell out "BOO".

Most dogs are playful. They put on a show.

My dog Tigger would jump around and
give you his paw just to say "Hello".

He was a funny dog who showed my family love.

Now I know he's sitting by God's side, up above.


Felicia (AKA) Feva

Printed in the United States
By Bookmasters